We Eat Together!

Hampton-Brown

School Publishing

Acknowledgments
Grateful acknowledgment is given to the authors, artists, photographers, museums, publishers, and agents for permission to reprint copyrighted material. Every effort has been made to secure the appropriate permission. If any omissions have been made or if corrections are required, please contact the Publisher.

Photographs: Cover GoGo Images Corporation/Alamy. **TP** Fotosearch/Photolibrary. **2** moodboard RF/Photolibrary. **3** (m) Frank Siteman/age footstock/Photolibrary, (mr) PhotoDisc/Getty Images, (br) Ljiljana Pavkov/iStockphoto. **4** (all) PhotoDisc/Getty Images. **5** Hill Street Studios/Blend Images/Jupiterimages. **6** Nick White/Jupiterimages. **7** (c) BananaStock/Jupiterimages, (r) Artville. **8** Jose Luis Pelaez Inc/Blend Images RF/Jupiterimages, (b) PhotoDisc/Getty Images. **BC** (tr) PhotoDisc/Getty Images, (br) Iconotec.

The National Geographic Society
John M. Fahey, Jr., President & Chief Executive Officer
Gilbert M. Grosvenor, Chairman of the Board

National Geographic School Publishing
Hampton-Brown
www.NGSP.com

Printed in the United States of America
Quad Graphics, Leominster, MA

ISBN: 978-07362-8371-7

19 20 21
10 9 8

NATIONAL GEOGRAPHIC
Reach™
Language • Literacy • Content

Unit 2	Language
Part 1	• Who is this? This is my _____ .
Part 2	• She/He is _____ .

Unit 2	Vocabulary
Part 1	• family members • food
Part 2	• actions • feelings

More Ideas

- Name foods and actions.
- Tell which foods you like.
- Give commands.
- Tell your own story!

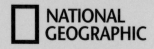

NATIONAL GEOGRAPHIC
School Publishing

■■ Hampton-Brown

ISBN 978-07362-8371-7

9 780736 283717

90000>

Pick a Plant!